this book belongs to:

_____

For My Mom

Thank you for always being my biggest fan and most loving, devoted supporter.
Love you always.

Hello, Swifties!

It's a dream come true to get to make these books for you and in return recieve the most amazing love and

appreciation. I pour my heart & soul into creating these pages for you to enjoy. I've absolutely adored seeing

all of your insanely beautiful, colored versions of each page from "You Need To Calm Down" Volume 1.

I look forward to seeing what you guys come up with for these all NEW pages in Volume 2!

For all the Swiftie "Clowns" out there, I added lots of little easter eggs to find. ;)

I hope you all enjoy every page of this book. It's made with love by a fan, for the fans. Happy Coloring!

> *If you feel the book you received has print quality issues (black isn't rich, stripes through pages, etc),
> please know this is an issue with Amazon's print-on-demand system and you can return it to them for a fresh, new copy!

Coloring Tips.

The paper in this book is perfect for color pencils, fine tip pens & alcohol-based markers. When using wet mediums, it's

recommended to use a blank sheet of card stock under the page you are coloring. Be sure to take advantage of the

color test pages in the back of the book to test your mediums, colors and shading before putting them on your page.

Enjoy your coloring adventure!

Follow, Share, Review & Spread the Word.

Sharing your masterpieces is encouraged! Follow me @CrazyDiamondStudio on Instagram and tag me in your finished

coloring pages. Colorists love to admire and be inspired by other's work. And if you love my book, kindly let me know

by leaving me a review on Amazon and share with all your Swiftie friends. It means the world to artists like me.

Follow me:

 @CrazyDiamondStudio

darling, i'm a
NIGHTMARE...

dressed like a
DAYDREAM

I HAD A
MARVELOUS
TIME...

RUININ'
EVERYTHING.

and i miss you, but...

i miss
Sparklin'

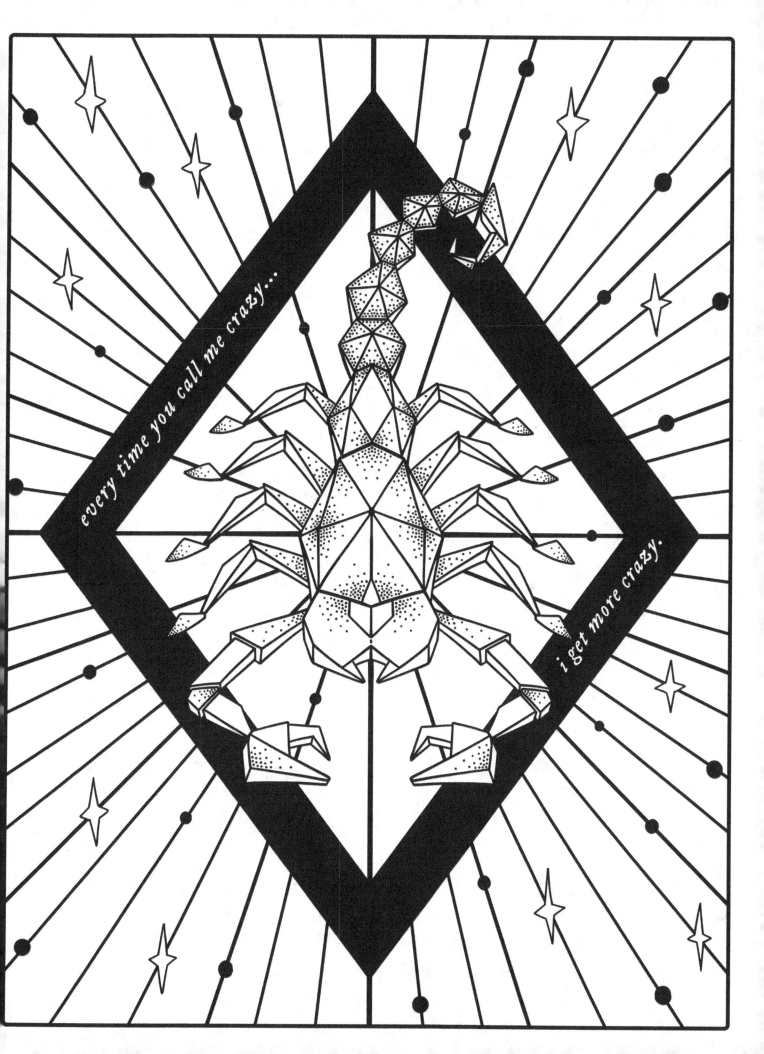

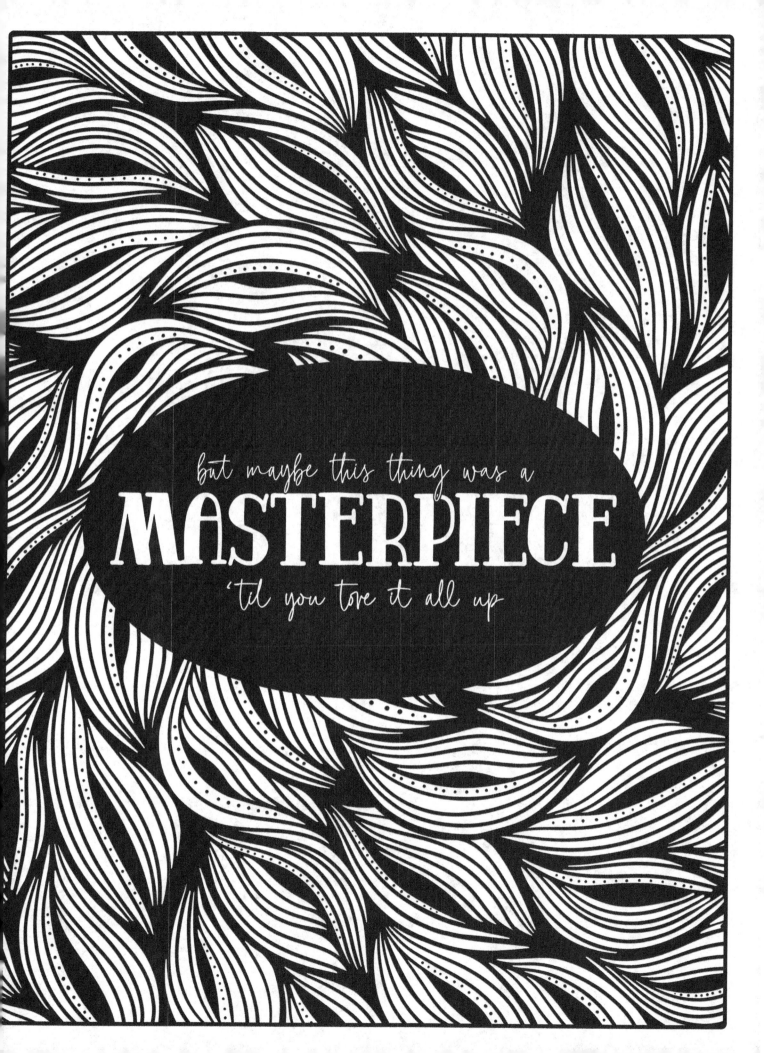

she'll patch up your tapestry that i shred

ALL MY FLOWERS GREW BACK AS THORNS

They're Gonna Crucify Me Anyway

· I KNOW PLACES ·
WE WON'T BE FOUND

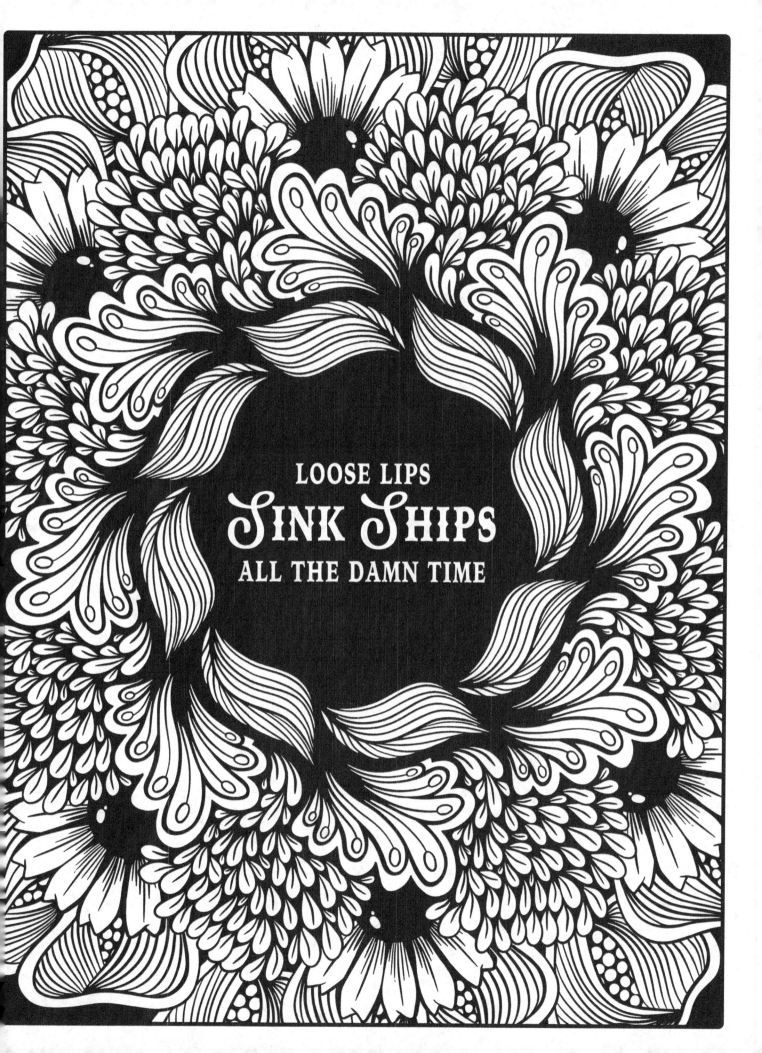

Color Test Page

Color Test Page

Color Test Page

Color Test Page

Color Test Page

Doodles & Ideas:

Doodles & Ideas:

Doodles & Ideas:

Thank You!

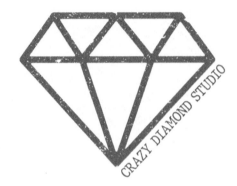

CRAZY DIAMOND STUDIO

Check out my other "Best Sellers" on Amazon!

'You Need To Calm Down' Volume 1.

Amazon "Best Seller"
Makes the best gift for Swifties of all ages! If you love this book, you'll love Volume 1 just as much!

'Can't Adult today'

Great for the snarkiest of colorists.
A little sass & a lot of snark paired with original hand-drawn, illustrations.
Makes a perfect gift!

'Empowering Quotes For Wild Souls'

Perfect for the Wild Souls of the world.
This book combines free spirited, empowering quotes with beautiful, hand-drawn illustrations.

Made in the USA
Monee, IL
05 November 2024

69306485R00052